AF413451

TIME TO PIVOT

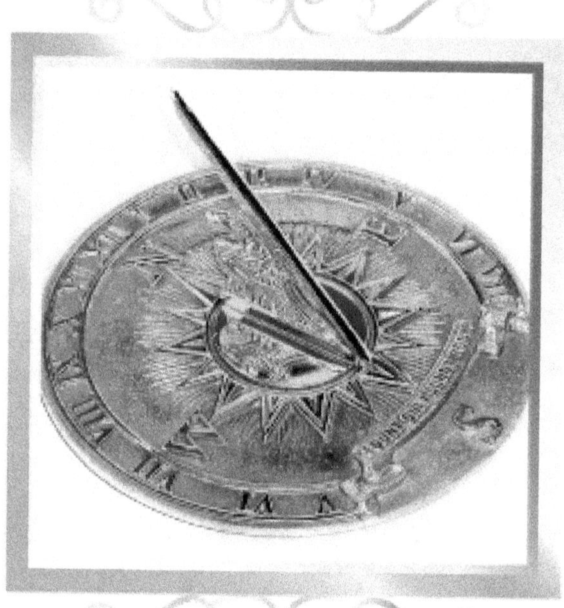

AND DO SOMETHING DIFFERENT!

PAULETTE SAMUELS

Time to Pivot
and Do Something Different!

DEDICATION

To my daughter, Tori, who gave me a whole different outlook on life. To my Unity Family, who taught me the truth about love and self, and to my friends, who encouraged me to place all my thoughts, inspirations and motivations in one place---

This Book.

Table of Contents

TIME TO PIVOT

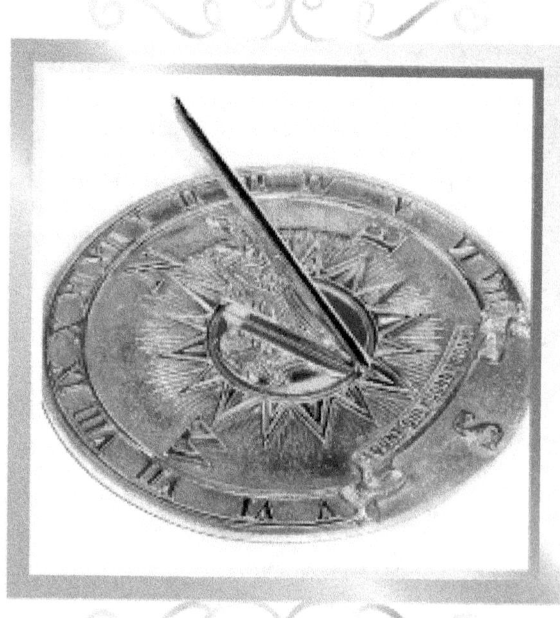

AND DO SOMETHING DIFFERENT!

PAULETTE SAMUELS

FOREWORD

In life, we all encounter moments that test our strength, challenge our resolve, and push us to our limits. It is in those moments of struggle and adversity that we find the opportunity to pivot and change the course of our lives for the better. In her new book, "Time to Pivot and Do Something Different," my dear friend Paulette Samuels shares her incredible journey of resilience, growth, and self-discovery, offering invaluable lessons that will empower and inspire readers to overcome their struggles.

I have known Paulette for over two decades, and throughout that time, she has been a constant source of support, wisdom, and inspiration. She is not only a friend but also a confidant—a person you can trust with your deepest fears and vulnerabilities. Her life story is a testament to her unwavering spirit, and it has left a profound impression on me.

In this book, Paulette lays bare her experiences, showing us how she navigated through life's toughest challenges and emerged stronger and wiser on the other side. Through her candid storytelling, we glimpse the highs and lows, the triumphs and setbacks, and the joy and heartache that have shaped her journey. As I read her words, I could not help but recall the times we cried together during the darkest moments, laughed together through the joyful ones, and supported each other during the most challenging trials.

It is a treasure trove of wisdom—a guide that will equip you with the tools to face life's uncertainties head-on and embrace the power of change. The nuggets of knowledge you will find within these pages will empower you to act, embrace your inner strength, and find purpose and joy in your journey of life.

"Time to Pivot and Do Something Different" offers more than just a glimpse into Paulette's life—it provides a roadmap for all of us to navigate our challenges and emerge as better versions of ourselves. Each chapter is a reminder that, no matter how difficult life may seem, there is always a path forward. Her resilience, authenticity, and determination will inspire you to embrace change, seize opportunities, and live life to the fullest.

As you turn the pages of this book, be prepared to have her move, uplift, and transform you into a new way of thinking. Her story will leave an indelible mark on your heart and soul, and her insights will resonate with you long after you have finished reading. I am confident that "Time to Pivot" will be a book you will cherish and return to whenever life throws its curveballs.

So, let us embark on this transformative journey together and pivot toward a future filled with courage, hope, and joy. When we embrace change and learn from our struggles, we unlock the true potential that lies within us.

Enjoy the journey, my friends.

Jacqueline Williams

INTRODUCTION

If you're feeling trapped in a relentless cycle and searching for an escape route, you've come to the right place. Here, you will embark on a journey of self-discovery and empowerment designed to boost your confidence, guide your path, and enable you to live the life that resonates most with your inner self—all while maintaining a deep sense of inner peace. It's time to challenge the notion that life is an endless struggle because it isn't!

Our existence is not meant to be marred by constant hardship and suffering. We aren't victims of a hostile world, nor are we pursued by unseen adversaries. The true battleground lies within our minds. The mind is an extraordinary instrument, yet our failure to harness its potential often leads to anxiety, fear, and, in severe cases, mental health challenges. What we must learn is to train our minds not to react impulsively to every external circumstance but to focus on nurturing our inner tranquility.

In today's fast-paced world, with countless distractions vying for our attention, we must exercise our innate power and rectify our thought patterns. We need to live the life we were destined for. It may be hard to believe, but we are far more capable than we give ourselves credit for. The misguided belief that we are inadequate keeps us trapped in a never-ending cycle of self-doubt. Remember, in life, everything has its moment. We are rushing toward the future, which closes our eyes to the beauty of the present. It's time to slow down, appreciate what surrounds us, and realize that gratitude is the key to unlocking more blessings.

When we lose touch with our inner selves, our efforts scatter, and we seek external validation and satisfaction. The ability to introspect, connect with our intuition, and listen to our inner voice becomes the compass we need to navigate our life's journey.

Now is the moment to shatter the constraints that confine us. Ignite your passion and enthusiasm. Learning to break free from the mold and shift our perspectives will liberate us from the chains that have bound our awareness, our thoughts, our health, and our overall well-being.

This book serves as a guide to kickstart your adventure, allowing you to reclaim your power and offering personal examples to help you connect with your authentic self. By doing so, you become a guiding light, attracting others to this path of self-discovery and empowerment. Let go of your inhibitions, break free, and live in awe of the beauty that envelops you.

Remember to breathe, meditate, laugh, love, and pray!

" When you talk you are only
confirming what you already know,
but when you listen you learn"

Dalai Lama's

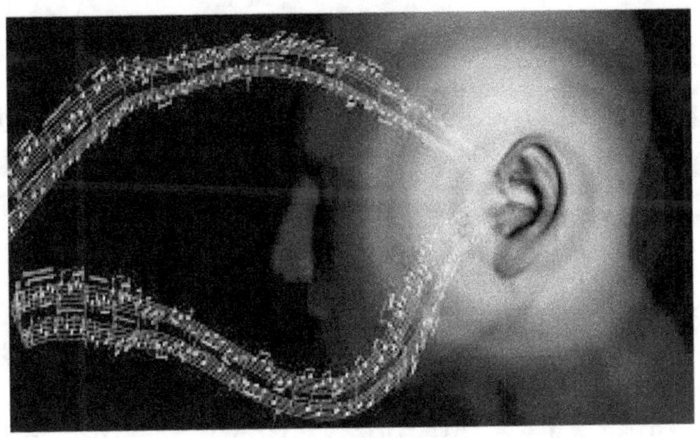

Chapter 1

<u>THE ART OF LISTENING</u>

Growing up, I was extremely shy and in no way talkative. Most people I know would find this hard to believe, but it is true! However, when I did speak, I was very witty. All that changed when I migrated from Jamaica to the United States. I found my voice and have not shut up since. Which is a good thing as I came out of my shell. Being talkative has drawbacks, especially when listening, as you want to get all your ideas and opinions across. I was the intellectual, current affairs consultant, and motivator type of gal who would try to get my point across to anyone who would listen. I gave a new meaning to the word "Loquacious." I remember my mom drilling in us, that we are born with two ears and one mouth, meaning we should listen more and talk less. Of course, that went over my head. As I got older, I became more conscious of her advice, but I continued to voice my opinions.

One might say that not listening started during our toddler stage, and that might be true because, in their mission to know themselves, listening is the furthest from a toddler's comprehension. Are we saying that toddlers' behavior spilt over into our adult lives? If so, we need to discard this mentality and act accordingly.

Society has not mastered the art of listening. It takes great skill to do so. Rather than listening to understand, we listen to respond.

Or, we have so much chatter going on inside our heads that we selectively listen to or tune out what is being said. I will be quick to point out that, at times, I fall into this trap, but I am becoming more conscious of how I use my listening skills.

We must understand that listening is a mutual understanding between a speaker and a listener. The three essential skills are triple listening, i.e., attitude, attention, and adjustment. Unbelievably, there is a difference between listening and hearing. We all listen, but do we hear or understand what is conveyed? A Finnish saying states, "Speech is silver, but silence is gold." If we should ask someone to repeat what was communicated, they could not, as they were either pretending to listen or cherry-picking what was essential to them. And, to get their point across, they talk over each other. Understand that non-verbal communication can be just as powerful. Remember, even the dull and ignorant, they, too, have a story. Everyone, for that matter, has a story, so be respectful and **LISTEN!**

ACTIVE LISTENING

Why do we feel that silence should constantly be interrupted by words? We are so good at chatter--everyone has an opinion and wants to be heard. The phrase "Silence is Golden" epitomizes what active listening is. Not every statement deserves a response. At times, silence is the answer. We need to become more fluent in silence. Active listening allows us to focus and have an open mind without judgment, observe verbal and non-verbal messages sent, and provide appropriate feedback as necessary. Usually, we have pre-planned responses as we would during a debate, thereby losing what the speaker is trying to convey, which is simply ignored. How about when we judge someone before they speak, only to find out that when they do speak, we are impressed by what they impart? Always focus on what the speaker is saying rather than using your thoughts to build roadblocks.

Active listening improves your communication skills, makes you non-judgmental, curtails biases and points of view, connects you on a deeper level, and builds trust.

How often do you think you know everything someone is about to say? Try to read their mind and complete their sentences. I have done this more often than I should, and I was surprised when the opposite was communicated. Other times we engage in conversations simply to win an argument, where we selectively listen to gather information to later use against the speaker. This happens frequently in business, politics, and media settings.

How about when you are engaged in a conversation but cannot get your thoughts across because you are constantly interrupted? We have all experienced this at some point. Either by someone who thinks they know it all or thinks that what you have to say is irrelevant. Rather than interrupting, we should visualize what the speaker is saying. Then, there are biases, especially against those with accents, who are dismissed because we refuse to take the time to listen and understand what they are trying to say. I have experienced this, and I do not have a strong accent. So, I empathize with those who do. A good listener will entertain every conversation; it is an effective way to understand that the speaker only expresses themselves on their terms. When in doubt, use nonverbal skills such as nodding and smiling, and avoid distracting movements. This will show that you are focusing. Not actively listening can eliminate you from future discussions or social interactions. No one wants to constantly fight with someone who refuses to listen or thinks they know it all. How do you practice active listening?

- Ask open-ended questions to be engaged and learn more.

- Paraphrase and summarize what the other person says to ensure you fully understand.

- Exhibit positive nonverbal communication like eye contact and leaning in.

- Avoid distractions and multitasking!

Other forms of listening: -

SELECTIVE LISTENING

This is the norm these days, causing so many misperceptions and distorted communications. Everyone who repeats a story twist it and relays it as they see fit. We constantly vied for who made a story more sensational or offered the best opinion. Study shows that an adult's attention span is about 8.25 seconds. We usually recall less than half of what we have heard (https://www.wyzowl.com/human-attention-span/)

DEEP LISTENING

From a spiritual standpoint, how often do we listen to our inner voice? Our intuition could be screaming at us, yet we turn a deaf ear. Because we are so prone to being in control, we usually ignore or question our inner voice. This has saved me from undesirable circumstances. We struggle with these uncomfortable situations because we refuse to listen as we are distracted, preoccupied, or forgetful. We use headphones to drown out noises but endanger our lives by not hearing what is happening around us. When it comes to our health, we get subtle warnings that something is awry, but we ignore them until they spiral out of control. Noise and distractions envelop us to the point where we *cannot appreciate peaceful surroundings. Listening to our inner voice is a struggle. We* tune out, *dismiss it, or find all the excuses not to face it. That still,* small voice is there to get your attention—it is your internal compass---your intuition. It is prompting you to act, and when you do not, the first thing you will utter is, "I should have followed my mind." Before seeking direction from the outer world, become still, turn inward, and listen to what your internal voice is trying to tell you. This form of listening also helps with Meditation and Manifestation, which allows you to slow down and tap into your intuitive thoughts. My inner voice and I are *constantly exchanging dialogues. I am so in tune with it that,* at times, I vocally talk aloud as if it is sitting across from me. "If you cannot hear, you will feel" is a phrase most West Indian parents repeatedly say to their children or anyone, which translates to "If you refuse to listen, you will have to face the consequences." I faced a few consequences, one of which was that my mom would wring my lips. I was upset then, but I thanked her now for giving me pouty lips and saving me from lip fillers.

IGNORING A SPEAKER

This happens for several reasons. You are either bored, think you have the answers, or impatient in hearing your story, which might be more important than the speakers. In our microwave society, we rush a speaker to "spit it out." Doing this not only lets you miss what is conveyed but also shows you up as a self-centered listener. Poor listening leads to misinformation, misinterpretation, and distortions.

BARRIERS OF LISTENING

Having information come at us at warp speed, demonstrating prejudice, or prejudging someone's speech and thought are our weakest communication skills.

UNWILLINGNESS TO LISTEN

Some refuse to listen. They are either stubborn or set in their ways. These folks believe their way is right and yours is wrong, or they do not feel they must conform to what you say—the "Knows It All." Research suggests that the average person hears between 20,000 and 30,000 words in 24 hours. The average number of words you can listen to per minute is around 450. Most people only remember about 17–25% of the things they listen to.

Consequently, listening to nagging or complaining for 30 minutes or more can cause damage to the part of your brain that manages problem-solving skills **(Charleysword.com)**

THE 70/30 RULE OF LISTENING

This is the ratio of listening vs. talking. **The rule of thumb is that 70% of the conversation is spent listening, and 30% is spent talking. Most people usually only** remember about 17-25% of the things they listen to. Try to utilize this rule the next time you are in a conversation--- listen **more than you talk (Proworkflow.com).**

If we take the time to listen, we will learn so much more than we already know. Take it from a talker! Changing my paradigm increased my knowledge immensely. Yes, I may still talk over someone, but it is not because I am being disrespectful; it is because my thoughts are bursting at the seams to get out. This, unfortunately, happens quite frequently in our society. We see it on talk shows and more so in debates. Opinions are flying at warp speed, and listeners are caught in the crossfire of making sense of what is presented, planning their escape route from this onslaught, and coming away with nothing substantial.

When we actively listen to others, we listen to our inner voice more intently. We are not aware that listening is a form of empathy. It is trying to see someone through their lens and connecting with their emotions. Emotions are not always as bad as one may think. Always focus on the speaker, wait your turn, and be engaging. If someone talks over you, continue talking because they will catch on and have no choice but to stop and listen---this is the epitome of force listening.

Types of Listeners:

- Pseudo-listeners - pretend to be listening.

- Stage Hogging listeners - making the conversation about them—playing the victim.

- Insensitive listeners – do not care about what you have to say. Very apparent in conflicting situations.

*****The above does not apply to those who are hearing impaired or those with disabilities*****

As humans, we are constantly engaged in various forms of discourse. Take a debate; for instance, there is always a back-and-forth dialogue and the competitiveness of who can outdo the other. Listening in this arena leaves the audience to cherry-pick what they can discern from this forum. Information is thrown at us at a rapid pace, and listening to understand is so fragmented that stories get distorted through various mainstream media. Social media, in turn, takes this information and further distorts it to divide and target specific listeners.

We must be respectful of anyone talking to us. For once, put yourself in a speaker's position. You would want whatever you are saying heard and folks are respecting your dialogue. In every relationship, listening is a challenge. You find that wives are always yelling at their husbands, "Are you listening?" Teenagers constantly battle with their parents, shouting, "You never listen to me," and toddlers are chased continuously by their mothers, pleading for them to listen.

Humor is another way of improving listening skills. Comedians show this to be true. You will notice that audiences pay attention to what they have to say. Even if the joke is unacceptable, They will sit there and listen to one joke after another until it resonates with them. Storytelling will also get people to listen. This will be what they remember about you, and you want to leave lasting impressions. Chris Tucker's "Can you hear the words that are coming out of my mouth" to get his co-star's attention was a classic listening skill—one we will remember for a long time. If you are at a conference, notice when the speaker starts sharing their life story that everyone perks up and pays attention. Because to get someone's undivided attention, you must make what you are conveying interesting. A monotonic dialogue will not only leave your audience wanting more, but eventually, they will tune out.

Then there is critical listening. Some occupations require a listening examination for you to qualify for a position. The first time I knew about this was when I applied to Continental Airlines for a Reservation Agent position, where I was placed in a soundproof room with a headphone to listen to the transmission of varying decibels of sound. Unbeknownst to me, I thought the louder it was, that I was on the right track. The opposite was true. If I heard a whisper, then my listening skills were on par---Of course, I was not accepted. There are other apparent professions, such as Air Traffic Controller, Emergency Dispatchers, Actors, and Lawyers, that also require critical listening skills.

As much as it is good to have excellent listening skills, we must be wary of what we listen to, as we can become victims of what is transmitted and thereby act on those impulses. These days, everyone has an opinion, and not everyone is worth listening to. Negative speakers will trap you in their web of downtrodden thinking or have you entrapped in their reality. Again, the media displays a lot of negativities, which causes us stress and fearful living. Their tagline, "If it Bleeds, it Leads," is enough to scare us out of our wits. Learn to decipher a speaker's intentions, listen intuitively, and act accordingly. Do not go down that rabbit hole. Listen to those you can learn from, who will uplift you and make you feel worthwhile rather than worthless.

Our alarm clock yells at us daily—a reminder to get out of bed. We listen, then snooze it, it yells again, and we repeat the process. We can use this exercise when someone is speaking, and we get the urge to interrupt---hit the snooze button and wait your turn. Notice how thunder and lightning, during a storm, are usually engaged in dialogue with each other? Both never talk at the same time; they wait their turn.

With all the noise and chatter around us these days, we have no choice but to listen. Listening is an adventure we will be on for our entire life. It will take you to places you never dreamed of. Start your listening journey now!

**" I'm not afraid of flying.
I'm afraid of not flying"...**

Anonymous

Chapter 2

<u>LIFE IS AN ADVENTURE</u>

Life is, as they say, a journey. We are not meant to stay in one place for too long. We work, partake in sports, and have and maintain a social life, family time, and extracurricular activities all to "Move it Along." The adventure begins at birth and ends in death—use this time wisely. Your journey should not be a weight on your shoulders. You should feel as light as a feather. You will encounter straight, rugged, or winding roads; your job is to learn how to navigate them. Life becomes a roller coaster because we are programmed to believe this is how life is, and we must comply. Everyone you meet on your journey also lives a complex life like you.

Learn to travel as much as you can, when you can, and as far as you can, using whatever mode you can. You are not a tree! Like a river, keep moving! Rivers sprint through valleys and villages, knowing their primary purpose is to get to the ocean---a bigger entity than itself. There is a vastness out there for you to explore. My love of travel saw me working part-time for a significant airline while attending college and working full-time. This experience taught me that whatever you want is attainable. "Once a year, go somewhere you have never been before" (Dalai Lama). The more you travel, the more difficult it becomes to stay still. I can attest to that, as I am always planning my next adventure on my return flights home. Time marches on---make the best of it as time waits for no one.

The curious will always seek out adventures. There is no greater knowledge than the world traveled. Through life adventures, you can create so many versions of yourself. Migrating to the United States was an adventure for me. Not knowing anything about the place I was going to make my permanent home proved that I was open to new experiences, curious about the culture I was adopting, and excited about new opportunities. Forty-three years later---what an experience! Do not rely on what people have to say about a place, take a trip there and come away with your own experience. Do not just travel to indulge yourself but also learn about yourself. You will always return from your adventures to a different person. Each time I return from a trip, the memory of where I visited is so strong, that thinking about it I am transformed back in time. You know that feeling when you get home and for the first few days you cannot stop reminiscing on all your discoveries, this is what it is all about. ***"Never get so busy making a living that you forget to make a life" (anonymous).***

I love to travel. I am convinced that it is part of my DNA. I will quickly get on a plane rather than drive cross-country in a car. I was once fearful of flying, but an unexpected turn of events changed all that. I was returning home in the late '80s after visiting my family. I was on standby for an overbooked flight. My aunt, who worked for another carrier, was on duty that night. Checking with her, I saw that those flights had no room—they were full.

What happened next opened a whole new world for me. I was frightened and excited simultaneously—if you can envision that feeling. Surprisingly, I traveled back home in the Cockpit. Never have I seen so many monitors, bells, and whistles above and in front of me. I sat in a jump seat next to the engineer (they were on flights back then). He assists the pilots with all aspects of the flight before takeoff. For the flight's duration, he taught me the basic operations of the flight deck and aviation, which helped ease my fear. This experience let me sit through turbulences without flinching and sealed the deal for my love of travel. It is the thrill of the adventure!

There is this misconception that flying is dangerous. Yes, travel anxiety is a thing. I was on a flight once from San Jose, California, to New York, and a female pilot stepped out of the cockpit to greet passengers. The guy sitting next to me dug into my leg so hard that it felt as if he had extracted blood. His fear was why a female pilot was flying our plane (how sexist!). The biggest fear passengers have is turbulence—the plane cannot fall from the sky. If you understand what keeps an aircraft aloft, then your fear becomes non-existent. While you can make an emergency landing without incident, you cannot abort takeoff at a Velocity 2 speed (the speed when a plane is about to lift) without catastrophic damage to the aircraft, serious injuries, or fatalities. Flying is one of the safest ways to get around. Statistics show that the chance of getting in a car crash is 1 in 5,000; the chance of being in a plane crash is 1 in 11 million (https://simpleflying.com/). Educate yourself about the flying process. Identify irrational thoughts. Learn to recognize triggers and practice relaxation techniques like deep breathing, visualization, and muscle relaxation. .

Taking a solo flight might be scary, but it is an exhilarating feeling when you finally take one. However, be vigilant! You may meet folks along the way, and you may strike up a conversation—do not divulge where you are staying or that you are traveling alone. And never, ever volunteer to ride, share, or accept a ride from a stranger, as they will know where you are staying. Solo travel is fun if you know how to maneuver the landscape—never let your guard down. Traveling with a group or with friends is ideal, but I have realized that the best-laid plans can go awry, and when this happens, it can become very frustrating when the entire trip is either delayed or canceled.

My first solo trip, at age 17, was to the Cayman Islands. I had no fear, as safety tactics were in place, telling folks I met that I was traveling with my parents, getting to know one or two natives, immersing myself in their culture, and ensuring I was always with a group of people. I am curious by nature, and solo trips opened a whole new world for me. During traveling solo in London, I met two young ladies who were staying at my hotel, and during our conversation, we found out that we were neighbors just a block away from each other. You never know who you might bump into in your neighborhood. One year, I did a great deal of solo trips and met so many acquaintances. At Christmas, my phone was ringing off the hook for a good six hours as they were all calling from different time zones. All calling to wish me a Merry Christmas. How exciting is that? For years, my parents were not aware that I was traveling solo. The look on their faces when they found out, made me question if I should refrain from doing it again, but adventure called, and the travel bug stung me so hard I had no other choice but to tend to my wound.

My daughter started her traveling journey at three months old. Yes, one would question that she would not remember anything at such an early age, but I was creative and kept a journal, written in the first person, along with photos until she was five. She looked back and was appreciative of those documented memories. 18 years later, we are still traipsing the globe. I guess, as you may say, she adopted my wanderlust. We also started our travel blog, https://younghearttravelers.com/ to share our travel adventures.

Do not hesitate to travel with your kids. There is so much for them to do these days in any location you are visiting. Traveling opens a wealth of knowledge and allows us not only to meet new people but also to learn about diverse cultures and become more tolerant. You can always make money, but memories from traveling will stay with you for a lifetime. We had a pandemic that put travel on hold for two-plus years. During the lockdown, I felt trapped in what I refer to as a country club prison. To feed my adventurous appetite, I did online virtual destinations, which helped me keep my sanity. So, you see, you can tailor your adventures to fit your needs. Airspaces and countries are now fully open, and people are again taking vacations. You do not have to travel far to be adventurous. Mini-vacations can be just as revitalizing. Life is just for living, and traveling is the best way to live a fulfilled life.

Throw caution to the wind. At least once a year, visit somewhere you have never been. The late Anthony Bourdain did just that by embarking on a culinary adventure around the World and in so doing, he not only sampled the cuisine but also immersed himself in the culture. He not only came back with a wealth of knowledge but was able to involve us in his journey through his weekly program, "Parts Unknown."

What is so shocking is that I am sure most of you have heard these excuses--"When the kids leave home, when I retire, or when I have enough money, I will start traveling." Do it now! There is no better time than now. What happens when you delay is that life will make different plans for you, and you will start lamenting what you wish you had. I know a lady who has lived in her State since she was born—she is now 75 and has never ventured out. She has never been on a plane or a train. To her, there is no reason to learn anything outside her comfort zone. There is no adventure there; that is a limiting mindset! When you live in this space, you will experience missed opportunities, limited achievement, and, above all, regret. Many people are just like her. If you do not want to fly, take a train, or drive to the next State, there is no telling what you will learn there. Create situations for yourself that will force you out of your comfort zone. You will return with knowledge of something you never knew existed.

If you look at it from a spiritual standpoint, it suggests that we Connect, Explore, Respond, and Grow. Being adventurous means exploring the unfamiliar. Always step out of your comfort zone and venture out onto the vast landscape we call the WORLD. We look at others having the time of their lives and start comparing their lives to ours. You are where you are for a reason. Find your adventure and build on it. You may be surprised that the folks you are comparing your life with want to be a part of your adventure. The less you know about the outcome, the more exhilarating it will be. Look at the birds; they have no limitations on where they go or how far. Toddlers are not afraid to explore what is around them and beyond. We should all develop this adventurous mindset. Start by exploring your city, looking up road trip options for cheap weekend trips, checking out off-season airline deals, and visiting friends or families. If you do not want to take a big adventurous leap, such as flying off somewhere, then start with trivial things such as cycling, hiking, watching the sunrise or sunset from strategic locations, kayaking down a river, or camping. Carve out a new route in your routine.

> Plan your travel six months in advance.
> Make a budget.
> Source out deals for your destination.
> Do your research.

Pay no attention to naysayers who want to curb your adventurous personality. I remember planning my trip to Dubai, UAE, and folks drilled me on why I was traveling to an Arab country. They even tried to deter me by insisting that I would have to cover my entire body and it was not a safe place for women. Well, I did go, and Dubai is the only Arab country closest to Western customs. Yes, there are rules that you must adhere to, but I did not have to cover myself except when I was entering a Mosque. Crime is non-existent as the punishment is severe. Every religion is practiced there; there are Catholic schools and all the modern amenities. I am sharing this so that no one will deter you from venturing out and confirming for yourself what others are negatively describing. Just do it safely!

Language barriers should not deter you, either. English is understood and spoken in most countries, and there is always someone to help you. What I discovered is that most natives want to learn English. On a trip to Spain, my friend and I were in a coffee shop, and these older ladies kept staring at us until they beckoned if they could join us. We gladly obliged. They spoke little English and told us if we did not mind, they wanted to sit and listen to us to hear our English. Well, we had such a good exchange and warmly embraced before parting ways. So, you see, as much as we think language is a barrier, we could be the ones to bridge the gap. Culture is not genetic; it is a learned behavior. Cross-cultural awareness helps to break down the barriers we build.

Life is one great adventure. Dare it. With all the changes, twists and turns, bliss, and grief that are thrown at us, we will either navigate them in the best way possible or become victims of anxiety, fear, and depression. To conquer life's anxieties, we must live in the moment, learn to enjoy our rest, and not become slaves to work. Giving your best at work is different from being addicted to work. Yes, it is part of the adventure, but it should not be the epitome of it. The same applies to taking care of your household, where you work hard to the point of burnout. Why would you not allow yourself to rest? Own and embrace the things that bring us joy. Always remember that the rock that is an obstacle in the path of one person becomes a stepping stone in the path of another. You know you have made the right choice when you have peace in your heart. Fill your life with stories to tell, not things to show.

Your beliefs are not real and can deter you from venturing out. You must correct your thinking to move forward. Thinking that it cannot create a limited mindset. Let your imagination evolve and take you on that journey that so willingly awaits. We do not always know where it will lead, but the thrill should keep you going. Trust the unlimited possibilities that are available to you. Do not let what others are doing deter you from taking that chance. Reflect on what you would like to be a part of.

Keep your adventurous wheel oiled and moving. The world awaits!

"Sometimes you have to Disconnect to Reconnect with Your Inner Self." – Dr. Nirvadha Singh

Chapter 3

<u>DISCONNECT TO RECONNECT</u>

As creatures, we need to feel connected. This begins at birth, when we are placed on our mother's bosom, and is where connectivity begins. It is this connection that will navigate us throughout our lives. Connection is good, as we need a sense of belongingness. However, we abuse this privilege and either become controlling, exhibit narcissistic behavior, or exhibit neediness. Letting go always seems to get the best of us. Fall is a great reminder to let things go. The trees display how beautiful it is to do just that. We will go to extreme lengths for acknowledgment, acceptance, and love. The need to stay connected is so strong that we lose ourselves in myriad ways to make this happen. We find it difficult to enjoy our own company. We need to schedule "Me Time'" to disconnect from others and unplug from our gadgets. If the pandemic has taught us anything, it is how to disconnect from things that do not offer any meaning to our lives, like unnecessary tasks and incessant chatter. Prioritizing the wrong things causes frustration and disappointment. My attestation to this is that I always put others ahead of my needs with the expectation that they would exhibit some gratitude. The disappointments I have had in life, and there are many, make me a much stronger and more forgiving person. I view these mishaps as learning curves and focus more on the lessons than the outcomes. When these events occur, the best reprieve is to turn to meditation and other forms of life balance techniques to connect with our inner selves. Set boundaries, learn to appreciate trivial things, pay attention to the birds chirping, something we do not give a second thought to practice more gratitude, set goals, connect with our spiritual being, and extend love to our fellow man. You may have heard of a "Gratitude Jar." I started this over five years ago, but instead of a jar, I created a folder in the note section of my phone labeled "Gratitude. I input everything I am grateful for each week. The best part is that on December 31st, I did a recap of all that I was grateful for throughout the year, and I can tell you that I had more to be grateful for than to complain about. Give it a try! You won't regret it.it.

Disconnecting becomes a task, so we feel that every given moment should be filled with some activity. In our society, it is the norm. Taking a vacation for some seems out of their reach, is not feasible financially, is a waste of time, or is motivated by the fear of missing out **(FOMO)** This mentality overpowers us. We have become creatures of habit. In other countries, the opposite is true. For one, they get more vacation time to disconnect, recharge, and reconnect. We can take a page from Finland's book, as they repeatedly take the vote for having the best quality of life. As a society, we work to the point of burnout. We work past our retirement age, and when we do retire, we end up not being able to enjoy the fruits of our labor. The sad part is that some even die in their first year of retirement.

We need to reconnect with our inner selves. Goodness is an attribute that we all possess, but we extend it to others and not much to ourselves. We tend to overextend our goodness to the point of people-pleasing. We accept being an option. Practice self-respect.

> ➤ Stop settling for less.
> ➤ Practice self-respect.
> ➤ *Always set boundaries.*

We spend a great deal of time chasing things that upset our peace. We do not meditate enough, pray enough, or practice affirmations enough. We do not talk much to each other anymore. We become prisoners of technology. We connect more with things that separate us from human contact. Our phones have replaced our watches—we cannot leave home without them, or we "feel naked." We lose track of time through the abyss called social media. It was aimed at bringing us together by connecting; instead, it has pulled us further and further apart from each other. Children as young as two years of age have gadgets shoved in their faces. Televisions are now retired babysitters—modern gadgets are the new norm. Their tiny brains are illuminated with bright lights and flashing objects moving across a screen. We find it ridiculously hard to disconnect from something so addictive that it seems a nuisance to reach out and make in-person connections. In Australia, a restauranteur produced a brilliant idea of placing a basket on each table requiring diners to place their phones in it and if they complete their meal without using it, they will get a 10% percent discount off their entire bill. In Japan, you cannot use your phone on trains. These countries are trying to bring back some semblance of what it was before technology took us hostage---minimizing personal interactions with our neighbors.

What we place importance on is not particularly important. Technology has infiltrated our society to the point where all attention is on what is staring back at us from a screen. Life is constantly happening in front of us, not on our screens. We realize that we are addicted when we misplace or leave our gadgets at home. Anxiety gets elevated. I cannot remember this much anxiety back when we forgot our watches. The pull to get back to our gadgets is extraordinarily strong. Social media has a stronghold in our society—back on overconsumption. We display our lives on this platform with such bravado as if it were a scene out of a Broadway play. Nothing is off-limits when it comes to posting. We view others' posts to see what they are up to or compare our lives to theirs. The technological connection is real. The decline in personal interactions and human connections is so strained that we find it hard, even in these settings, to pull ourselves away from our gadgets. Is social media usage damaging to real-life interactions? To a degree, yes! Our gadgets (phones, tablets, etc.) have a stronghold on us. The humans around us are almost nonexistent. Text Messages, WhatsApp, and Messenger have hacked inter-personal communication. If we are not on any of these platforms—we might as well be invisible. Facebook, Instagram, Twitter, TikTok, and YouTube are just as addictive. These apps can suck you into a state of time-wasting videos, pictures, and articles. The great comedian George Carlin refers to them as "digital petting zoos." We are constantly looking down at our phones and forgetting picture-taking; we have become paparazzi caught up in sensationalism. Understand that you are not living in the real world---you are living in a digital world.

We find it so hard to disconnect from the digital world, but if we take the time to think of the effects it triggers, namely comparison with others and raising doubts about your self-worth, which can potentially lead to mental health issues such as anxiety and depression, we would minimize its use. Do not continue down this abyss. Most who are profiling are having more problems than they let on. Refrain from letting digital life interrupt your reality. For them, this platform is their form of escapism. Pay no attention to appearances, as they are not real. Hozier states that "Social **Media is** an advertisement for the superficial, extroverted Self." Researchers found that 29% of girls who spent three or more hours per day on social media engaged in self-harm, and 31% of girls who spent five or more hours on social media were depressed (https://www.jec.senate.gov/). As for selfies—another addictive application---do they increase self-confidence or self-centeredness? Filters on Apps such as Instagram and Snapchat force others to resort to cosmetic surgery—mirroring filtered versions of their perfect selves—a big issue among teenagers, which can also lead to violence by their peers. We are no longer seeking validation from our parents. Instead, we allow these Apps and strangers to take on this role. We should not allow digital life to interrupt our reality.

Taking time for ourselves is extremely hard in our "Hurry up and Wait" society. Why do we need to fill every spare moment? We question everything, and we overthink to the point of depression, thereby disrupting our lives. Why do we become prisoners? We do not set boundaries or set aside time for ourselves. I was there and wanted to take care of everyone and everything. I felt drained, and I realized that I must disconnect from some of these tasks to reconnect with a better way of life. Setting boundaries is crucial. But the hectic pace of our daily lives interferes with us, slowing down not only our physical routines but also our mental chatter. Your life is what you make it. You must visualize your goals, seeing the end from the beginning.

We look at others and aspire to be just like them, and nothing is wrong with that if you remove comparison from the equation. You are who you are—no more, no less—and you should embrace that. What you see in others is already in you, and you will eventually attract it to you. A negative mind cannot bring about positive thoughts. Both thoughts cannot occupy the same space. You must decide which is more beneficial to you. We are all faced with challenges, but you are responsible for the way you accept and deal with them. No one can harm us unless we allow them to, no one can think for us unless we let them, and no one can let us feel less than—it is all up to us to decide what we will allow.

There is a significant difference between being alone and being lonely. We are quick to think that we are unlovable, but when you fully love yourself, there is no need to fight or search for someone to complement you. We must love ourselves before we can love someone else. We struggle with self-love. It took me a while to understand what this was. For me, it was being there and sharing love with everyone around me because I had enough to go around. I realized that this was always short-lived, and I would be disappointed as the love I extended did not get reciprocated. Aspiring to always have someone in our life or a crowd in our midst is a want, not a need. The soul will attract what it needs—no need to hurry up the process. Going against this will only lead to frustration and disappointment. We must take responsibility for our experience. Stop self-judging! Return to your true self by not buying into what others feel about you. Our creation is out of love, and we must keep this thought in mind to fully experience our full being.

In life, when we disconnect from what does not matter or what is not important, we get to a place of peace and enlightenment. You will develop...

> Self-confidence,

> Self-esteem

> Self-love

> Self-awareness

Self-confidence is where, in your innermost being, you become confident in yourself. You must build tenacity. Pay attention to the person you see when you look in the mirror. Repeat positive words to yourself until your subconscious mind accepts them.

Self-esteem is believing in your character as a person. Prove it to yourself, not anyone else. Being able to step out and take risks. Being honest with yourself.

Self-love is loving your body, soul, and spirit the way God created you.

Self-awareness is being aware of who you are, where you are going, and what you want to do with your life. Pay attention to your surroundings and respond accordingly.

There is so much information aimed at us, like daggers, that the brain can only absorb so much. Paying attention to what is relevant to our well-being will eliminate what is unworthy, allowing us to monitor our thoughts. We do not pay attention to our thoughts. Change your thoughts, and you will change your reality. We must live in our truth, practice integrity, and embrace the thought process. Our behavior will determine what we receive. Disconnect from what does not serve you. Take yourself off "Autopilot." The choice you make determines the life you will live. We are creatures of habit who keep repeating the same routine over and over and rebel at the least bit of change from the norm. Experience will teach us a valid lesson, and we must take responsibility. Our desires will determine what we choose to partake in and what we choose to dismiss. We can choose to live a life of fear, anger, negativity, and malice, or we can choose faith, calmness, positivity, and love. We always have a choice. The universe always sends us what we need to learn in advance; at times it is even staring us in the face, but we shrug it off and carry on in our old ways. Taking responsibility is the first step in owning our feelings. Emotional intelligence plays a crucial role in how we interact with others.

➢ Learn to control our impulses.

➢ Practice self-awareness

➢ Exhibit empathy

➢ To be respected and valued for what we say and think.

Without these, we are just moving along like a blob in the universe.

We are now in a time where those who speak their truth get disrespected, and liars are applauded and embraced. No matter the circumstance, always speak and remain true. What we tell ourselves is what we believe in ourselves. You cannot be a half-liar and a half-truthteller; either you are a liar or someone who speaks the truth. Unlike a liar, who will always have to remember the previous lie and build on it, telling the truth will set you free.

" We need to do a better job of putting ourselves higher on our own " to do list."

Michele Obama

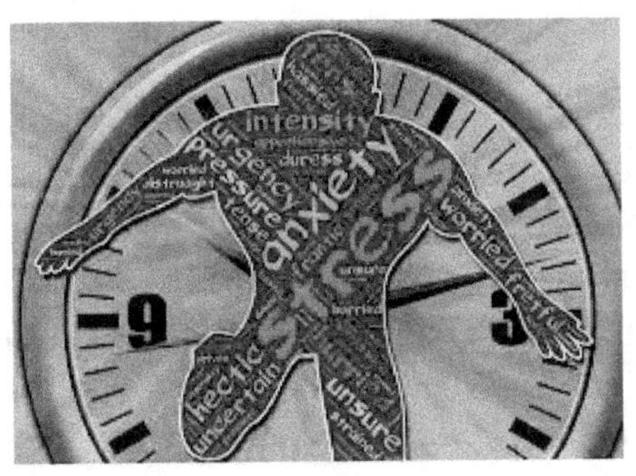

Chapter 4

<u>WHAT DRAINS YOUR SPIRIT DRAINS YOUR BODY</u>

How many times do we end the day fully exhausted? We spend most of our time working so hard that work/life balance is something that we struggle to aspire to. Our to-do list is a mile long and most of the time we are not even included. How about creating a "Don't Do List" instead of trying to complete your endless "To Do List"? Being everything to everyone is taxing not only on the mind but also on our physical being. We serve others because we feel it is expected. Do not shrink yourself to let others feel secure around you. Scheduling daily downtime, doing things that boost your spirit, and partaking in things we love are sure ways to manage and get a handle on work/life balance. Stop doing things to get approval or love. Stop being everything to everyone. You are only one person. If you are always giving but not gaining anything in return, then you are just people-pleasing. Surprisingly, we tend to judge ourselves very harshly. There is always this feeling of inadequacy or the feeling that we will be chastised for not taking care of others. These self-deprecating thoughts play mental Olympics in our minds. Negative emotions consume us. We fail to put ourselves first. We were not placed on this earth to struggle or be unhappy. Contact the core of your being. Once you do, your ego has no chance of consuming you. Life is not fair, but we need to own our feelings and stop judging ourselves. We need, at times, to give up something to gain something better. You cannot build a plane and fly it at the same time. That is, you cannot entertain positive and negative thoughts at the same time. Work on being around positive people, speaking positive words about your life, and thinking good thoughts. Learn to live in the moment. That is without fear, people pleasing, and seeking validation. Make each day count. Keep a gratitude journal. We are always told to get a life, but life is not something to get--- it is something to express. We cannot give what we do not have. In life, you should do something so good and profound that you will want to constantly repeat it. Learn to inhale peace—exhale love.

Once you start living a life of love instead of fear, you will find that your stress level decreases, and you start saying good things about yourself. There is no wrong or right way. Developing a positive state allows you to train your brain to see the good in everything; it helps you to learn from your mistakes but not let them define you; it increases your self-awareness; it helps you manage your stress; it allows you to own your feelings, and eventually, it allows you to develop a spiritual connection. Overthinking is a negative emotion, and negative emotions will consume you if you do not get a handle on it. I always affirm that we should refrain from paying attention to appearances, as they are unreal. "We do not see *things as they are, we see things as we are.*" (*The Talmud*). We all envision destinations as places; there is a newer way of perceiving things---PIVOT!

We continue to struggle with self-love, and even though we know it is necessary, we tend to dismiss it. We have all been programmed to believe that we are not pretty enough, not intelligent enough, and not good enough. Society manipulates us to conform to specific standards, and we gladly oblige. We need to shift ourselves away from other people's opinions. We take care of our children, our parents, and our spouses to the point where there is little time left for us. We tend to think it is selfish not to take care of others and put our needs on hold. We overcompensate in every area of our lives. See, we have been so conditioned that it is hard to **break the chains**. Females, because of their nature and nurture abilities, fall prey to this norm more than the male species. Love is something that we all yearn for. However, it is something that we already possess, but what do we do? We seek it with reckless abandonment of the external and, in so doing, eradicate self-love. To develop confidence and self-love, we must start with ourselves. Start with the trivial things and build from there. Your body alarm will blare when you are not taking care of yourself. It is a reminder that you need to become centered and reclaim your power. Ask for what you want—The universe will give you, with exact precision exactly what you ask for—nothing more, nothing less. Recognize your worth and claim it! Once we discern what we can and cannot control it will alleviate depression, stress, and anxiety.

We must learn to recognize the types of people that come into our lives and try to dissociate ourselves from them. You know the ones, the user who only finds/knows you when they need something, the complainer, always dragging you into their negativity/drama, the blamer, who is always blaming everyone else but themselves, the gossiper, who always has someone else's story to spill, and the competitor, who is always trying to outdo you every chance they get. These are people who will ruin your life. Self-love and self-care must be your priorities. Stop feeling inadequate. Let your light shine. If you do not have self-love, you will fall prey to predators and narcissists. Develop a relationship with yourself so that when you extend yourself to someone else, if it is not reciprocated, you lose nothing. Do not let anyone suck the wind out of your sail. You are on a mission, and the horizon awaits. then you lose nothing. Do not let anyone suck the wind out of your sail. You are on a mission and the horizon awaits.

Let go of pride and ego. Pride goes before a fall, and ego is an elevated belief that you can handle any situation, even if it is destroying you. The unwillingness to forgive is usually our ego taking center stage. Train yourself to keep your ego in check. Live your life fully! Take that trip, even if it is solo, purchase that bag you had your eyes on, and meet up with friends who uplift you. Go with the flow instead of going against it.

- ➢ For 30 minutes a day, be still and quiet your mind.
- ➢ Do 5-10 minutes of affirmations every morning.
- ➢ Practice meditation, manifestation, and yoga.
- ➢ Focus on that which connects you with your authentic self. Strive for it!

We tend to conform to the wrong things, like the constant battle in our minds, yearning for the perfect life or the perfect body, and trying to live up to societal standards. We must be willing to change our attitudes, our minds, and our reactions. You must develop a strong belief that you are enough—that no one can be like you. You are divinely made!

How often do we find ourselves trapped in this state of people-pleasing? Not everyone will like you. Be yourself! We tend to seek validation at every opportunity and complain when it is not addressed. This is quite evident on social media. How people treat you is how they think about themselves. Rather than complaining, work on positive self-talk and daily improvement. Complaining only gives you more stuff to complain about. Challenge yourself by keeping a mason jar of your complaints. Try to go for a week without complaining, and each time you complain, you need to place that complaint in the mason jar. If your jar gets filled at the end of the week, then you have some issues that must be addressed. It is not an easy task, but it will confirm that complaints attract more things to complain about.

Negative thoughts cloud our judgment on whether we should do pleasant things for ourselves. But why do we hold on to negative stuff? Is it:

- ➢ To Play the victim?
- ➢ To Seek sympathy?
- ➢ To Manipulate or be in control?

> ➤ An act of Stubbornness or vindictiveness?

The human brain gives more weight to negative experiences than positive ones. Hanging onto negativity is very exhausting. It is more beneficial to accentuate the positive and eliminate the negative. A study done by the Boston University of Medicine states that:

> ➤ Positive thinkers live longer than negative thinkers.

> ➤ Positivity leads to better cardiovascular health and boosts immunity.

> ➤ A positive attitude improves outcomes and life satisfaction across a spectrum of conditions, including traumatic brain injury, stroke, and brain tumors.

A lot of us would take positivity more seriously if we paid attention to this correlation. No matter how difficult a situation is, there is a positive aspect embedded in it. See the good in everything. Find it and focus on it. We look around and wonder why others are always happy and upbeat. It is not that they are not faced with trials and tribulations, but it is that they refuse to give negativity any power. This is a vital part of self-love---reclaiming your power. When fear creeps in, try to take time to breathe. Start your day off right. Apply the brakes on the rat race. Develop an attitude of gratitude. You attract what you are. Be kind to yourself and others. People around us are hurting and need love and encouragement. Do not be insensitive. Be a pillar of support and a beacon to those in need. Let your light conquer the darkness that surrounds us. Train your mind to process things as if they are not what you intend them to be. This microwave way of thinking, where we want everything done in a "micro-second," is what is creating the most damage. We fail to take the time to slow down. I am no different, but I am getting better at this. My daughter keeps reminding me that the world is not going anywhere, so why the rush?

We have a choice, just like the trees and flowers in the spring, to positively renew ourselves. When we think positively, we project it into the world for others to enjoy as well. Positiveness will attract what you desire in your life. Whatever you prepare for, through your mindset, you will be placed in that situation. Eliminate negative self-talk from your vocabulary. Negative vs Positive examples:

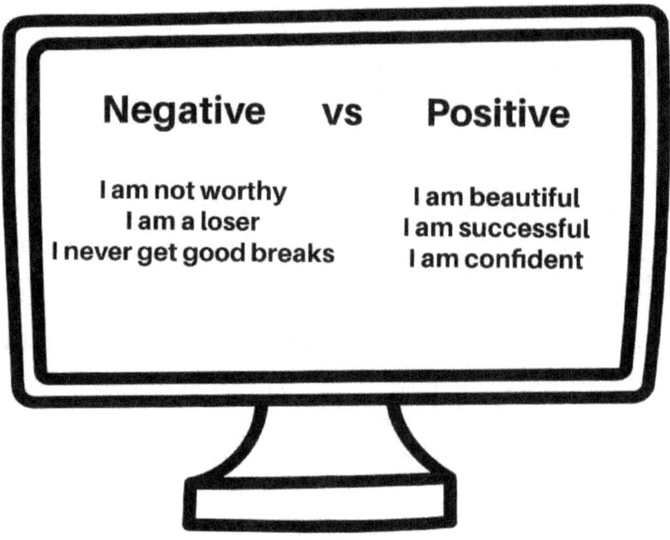

Make a concerted effort to surround yourself with positive people. Have you noticed how draining it is to be around negative folks? They have a problem for every solution. Toxic relationships are suffocating. Fight the feeling of becoming a victim! Do not be hard on yourself. Understand that what is inside you is greater than any external force. Learn to raise your vibrations. When asked how you are doing, instead of saying, "I'm fine, say I am great," as you want to attract greatness to yourself. Everyone is going through something, even if it is not shared. Reflect on your life and savor the moments that bring you joy; think of your mistakes as life lessons to do better and grow stronger from your sufferings. You must choose what to accept and what to let go of. When you learn to ignore, you become less irritated. If you are easily irritated, then you can be easily manipulated. Not every action deserves a reaction. Fall in love with being the best version of yourself. Learn to live a full and rich life.

Forgiveness is one thing that we find hard to do or, better yet, do not fully understand how it works. Forgiveness is limitless. Forgiving someone does not mean that you agree with what they did; it is freeing yourself of the bond that came out of the situation. The phrase "You should forgive but never forget" is holding you hostage. You must forgive fully for your spirit to be rid of the burden. By choosing not to forget, you are still hoarding it in your subconscious, which can resurface at any given moment. Oftentimes, the person you are not forgiving is going about their merry way, not even giving you a second thought while you are replaying the scenario repeatedly and sharing it with anyone willing to listen. We must rid ourselves of this debilitating course of action. Notice how lighter you feel when you genuinely forgive yourself and someone else? The term "Let go and Let God" means taking your hands off the situation and allowing him to handle it. The same would apply to letting him fight your battles. Do not feel guilty for doing so. Guilt does not correct anything. What it does is it gnaws away at your peace. We must love often, forgive more, and live a life filled with peace and integrity.

Why do we worry about things we have no control over? I can relate to this. I was a worry wart. I would worry for you even if you were not worried for yourself. This took a toll on my sleep pattern, my mood, my health, and my stress level. I had to force myself to get out of this conundrum. I am happy to say that I have transformed into a different person. Yes, we can get concerned about things, but we should not let it consume us to the point where we get overly anxious. Anxiety, of course, comes from us wanting everything to go well, and if it does not, then it is an indication that we should give up the fight. Worrying interferes with your confidence and self-worth. It hinders you from moving forward. We are constantly labeling ourselves negatively—I am too fat, not pretty enough, etc., a form of appearance management, no less. We are in this constant tug-of-war with our thoughts, which only heightens our fear factor and hinders us from positively facing life. We must be confident in our approach to life. Understand that what you think is working against you is working for you. Not every one of your desires will be fulfilled, and once you acknowledge that, life becomes easier to manage. Your thoughts and emotions are what drive your actions. You must be willing and ready to take risks and transform yourself.

Transforming yourself is not possible without honesty. We want the transformation but are not honest with ourselves. We tend to tuck neatly away what we do not want others to know about. Sometimes, you must give up something to gain something—positive and negative thoughts cannot occupy the same space simultaneously. Consider what changes you must make to start this journey. Setting goals is the template for achieving your transformation. Specific efforts must be enforced to prepare for what you want.

"The Only Way to Follow Your Path
is to Take the Lead"

- Joe Peterson

Chapter 5

<u>LEAD YOUR WAY</u>

Many can manage, but a few of us can lead, and there is no truer statement than this. What does it mean to lead? To lead is to take the initiative in what you want to accomplish by setting attainable goals and following through. It is not about you but about the people you serve. Many of us can be leaders and good ones at that, but when it comes to our lives, we fall short. I am always ready to help others with their leadership goals, among other things, but I seem to place my needs on the back burner. Why is that? Is it that we manage others better than ourselves, push ourselves into the background, or believe that leadership only pertains to others? Well, I have learned that I have the potential and am more than capable of leading the way. Understanding that this is not a selfish act is the first step in taking control of it. When we are at a crossroads or hit roadblocks, rather than figuring out the best solution, we engage others to help us. Nothing is wrong with seeking help or advice; most leaders do this anyway, but the bottom line remains with us. That is, we must take the lead and make a viable decision that fits our challenge.

Having a voice propels you to lead your life. It does not matter whether you are an introvert or an extrovert; what matters is that you let your voice be heard. How many times have you doubted yourself only to find that your ideas and opinions, when shared, were fully embraced? Doubting ourselves is a sure bet to leave us paralyzed at these crossroads. You may have heard the term "have a voice at the table." What that is telling you is to stand up for yourself and what you believe in. It is vocalizing your thoughts and authentically expressing yourself. Being shy is not an excuse for not expressing yourself or leading the way. No two voices are the same. Everyone has something to say and should vocalize their thoughts. Not doing this, you fall into the trap of going with the flow—in essence, being a follower. Followers accept things forced on them that they do not want to do. They are easily brainwashed or manipulated. The sad part is that we are programmed to be followers. A toddler is a fine example; they mimic everything we say and do and are constantly rewarded for displaying such an act. Teenagers and adults alike also follow what their friends are doing—a form of peer pressure. So, at times, the task of breaking away from these norms becomes daunting.

Copying what others do does not help. Doing it blatantly or secretly brings about the same effects. There is a saying that people try to copy others, not knowing that everyone is presented with a different exam. "You were born an ***original, don't die a copy" – John*** Mason

Leading yourself can be difficult, which is why most of us avoid this task. What it does is force us to take stock of what is going on in our lives without judgment or criticism, and it helps bring about clarity on what we are experiencing. It is easy to point out others' imperfections, but the ability to see our own becomes challenging. You cannot lead others unless you first learn to lead yourself.

Everything begins with the Self.

- ➢ *Self-discovery*
- ➢ *self-awareness*
- ➢ *self-acceptance*
- ➢ self-growth.

You must practice self-leadership, which means being responsible for your own life. When we understand and practice self-leadership, we develop more confidence and resilience. Always incorporate the 3 Cs of self-leadership....

> ➢ Connection
> ➢ Confidence
> ➢ Competence

Struggling to speak or remain silent is the biggest barrier to leading your way. You are uniquely made, and we all have talents. Act on them! We spend a lot of time focusing on what others are doing and becoming envious of or desiring what they have. Row your boat—be the captain of your ship. Do not succumb to self-pity by looking down on yourself. You have overcome challenges before. Keep your head high! Aim for greatness! Time to PIVOT!

Most of us, in our careers, are leaders for others and have different leadership styles. These leadership styles are not just obvious in the business world but are obvious in other daily settings.

> ➢ Autocratic
> ➢ Democratic
> ➢ Laissez-faire

<u>Autocratic</u> – This group is usually persuasive and makes all decisions. While this is not a bad trait, especially in a crisis or when quick decisions are needed, the downside is that this form of leadership can lead to micromanaging.

<u>Democratic</u> – This group ensures that everyone on the team understands what is required and ensures that their initiatives and suggestions are part of the decision.

<u>Laissez-faire (French for "Let it Go")</u> – This group exhibits a hands-off approach, giving team members full autonomy over their work. Those who are self-motivated thrive well under this leadership. The drawback is that inexperienced members struggle to find their way. Also, this form of leadership does not lead by example.

Most of us worked with or encountered leaders who possess one or more of these traits. To us, the ideal leader can juggle each of these and make them effective for those who work for them. We have heard horror stories, and I have witnessed a few. I worked in an office where a manager threw whatever he was drinking at his assistant when he did not get his way, or another who caused his team members to tremble when he entered a room. The climate for leaders has changed drastically. Gone are the days when these types of behavior would get a slap on the wrist. Organizations have become stricter in handling these behaviors and make no bones about terminating leaders who do not adhere to these new company policies. "Leadership is about making others better because of your presence and making sure that impact lasts in your absence." (Sheryl Sandberg)

Men have been leaders in the workplace and other professions for as long as we can remember, and we have grown accustomed to it. However, at the turn of the 20th century, more women joined the workforce and assumed leadership roles. Women have been leaders all along—just not in an office setting. The fact that they raised children, managed the household, and made decisions that benefited the family speaks volumes. There are now fewer stay-at-home moms than ever before. Women have attained leadership roles such as Heads of State, Presidents, Prime Ministers, and CEOs of Fortune 500 companies while still handling their family roles. A study shows that women now surpass men in college degrees by almost three to two (Pew Research.org). Now that they have a seat at the table...what is next? They have demonstrated that they are no longer going to sit and play dumb or be silenced when they have an opinion.

To be in this seat of opportunity, they must be present and ready. In other words, carve out their way. Men and women view leadership differently. Men have had this role for so long that, at times, they view women leaders as incapable. Why is that? Is it because women view professional advancement differently, or do they feel threatened? Women, overall, possess stronger leadership traits, namely (www.replicon.com/blog).

> *Inclusivity*

> *Empathy*

> *Encourage Free Thinking*

> Teamwork. ...

> Good at *Multitasking*. ...

> Motivated by Challenges

> Value Work/Life Balance

Because of these views, their climb up the corporate ladder becomes a struggle. The stigma attached to these traits is that women are.....

> *Are not assertive in negotiating pay raises or promotions.*
> *Not building alliances— (Men know how to play this game).*
> *Unequally treated.*
> *Leadership qualities are questionable....*

  o *Strong and Confident---not likeable*

  o *Softer style—likable but incompetent*

> *Placing family responsibilities over a career path*

How do we explain these challenges? Compared to men, women are...

> *Tasked with multiple life goals.*

> *Placed less importance on power-related goals because of their life goals.*

> *May view high-power positions as having negative outcomes.*

Women are often underrepresented in most high-level positions in organizations. Much research has provided evidence that bias and discrimination cause and perpetuate gender disparity. Although we are seeing a bit of progress here (Diversity, Equity, and Inclusion initiatives) it is still not enough to move the needle to where it should be. We should not let fear hinder our ability to lead. It immobilizes you and keeps you stuck with being less than you are. Standing up for yourself, although a daunting process, must be pursued with due diligence. We often hold back because we feel intimidated, fearful of repercussions, and do not want to be viewed as aggressive or shy. Do not fall prey to Imposter Syndrome. Imposter Syndrome is...

> Feeling *like a "Fraud"*
> Thinking you are not capable of doing what you are assigned to do.
> Fear of asking questions may be viewed as not smart.
> *That you are not* worthy of your success.

Why are women good at managing but fearful of leadership? "Management is about persuading people to do things they do not want to do, while leadership is about inspiring people to do things they never thought they could." (Steve Jobs). This should be a mantra for those who question their capability. The fear of success is stronger than the fear of failure. What we fail, no pun intended, to realize is that failure is part of the journey to success.

The race to success and leadership comes with various hurdles, setbacks, and discouragements. Good leaders focus on the following:

- ➤ Cooperation instead of competition
- ➤ Harmony instead of discord
- ➤ Unity instead of separation
- ➤ Inclusion instead of exclusion

Not everyone can attain the above, but the aim is to incorporate them into your leadership goals.

When it comes to leadership, women are usually labeled "overthinkers" (men fall into this category as well) and are denied working on projects that require a quick turnaround. Situations such as this are perceived negatively, are excluded, and are discriminated against. We cannot allow ourselves to be ruled by emotions and say or do something we might regret. No matter the circumstance, do not overreact---remain calm. You need a greater perspective before making decisions. Just affirm the following: "None of these things move me," and "I am not going to let ***other's opinions*** ruin my peace." You will be surprised at how these phrases can make a world of difference in how you react in challenging situations. We tend to give our all to whatever we are tasked with, but we must understand that there is a difference between doing something genuinely and doing it to please others or for a sense of belonging. People- Pleasing consumes us as we tend to apologize for things that do not warrant an apology; we overcommit to projects, plans, and responsibilities; we overexplain things to keep the peace; and we feel guilty when we take time for ourselves. Learn the art of saying no. Do not make excuses or overexplain yourself. ***JUST SAY NO!***

Learning this balance takes practice and determination. I was told once by a principal that leadership in the business world and the educational world are completely different----not so. Leadership has specific components in how it is carried out. There is no set rule for one and not the other.

Leaders should take into consideration when managing others that……

> ➤ People leave managers, not companies.
> ➤ Managers cannot only look after *themselves—where their* bottom line is their performance and bonus.
> ➤ Narcissistic *tendencies – belittles and threatens.*
> ➤ Treating people like numbers – viewed as expenses, not assets (burnout, stress, etc.)
> ➤ Excessive *Control - micromanaging*
> ➤ *Taking the Spotlight from the team—taking the credit for others' success*

These behaviors bring about conflicts. Learning to manage effectively, not overreact, and adapt to changes is the best alternative for guiding others. Take responsibility by cultivating resilience.

Overall, if you are navigating life or leading others, there is no better time than now to **PIVOT AND *LEAD YOUR WAY!***

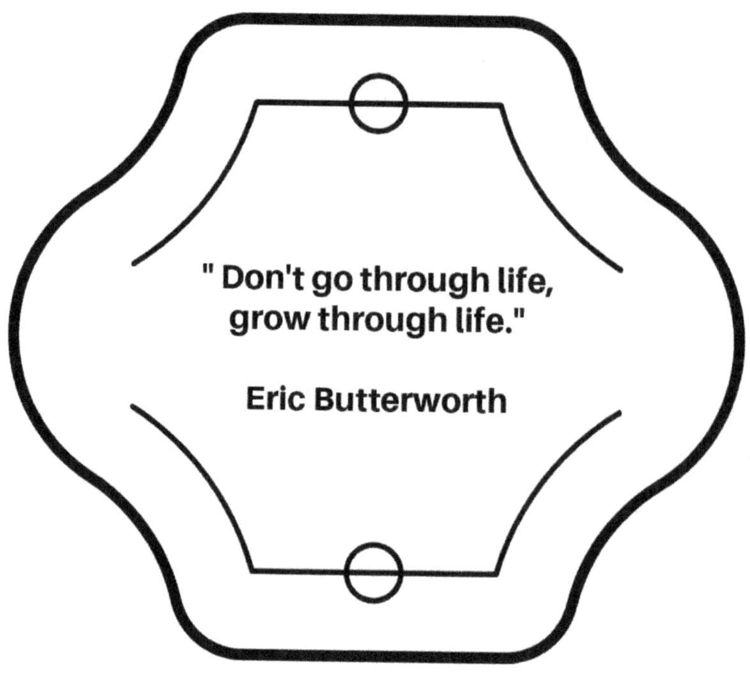
" Don't go through life,
grow through life."

Eric Butterworth

Chapter 6

LIVING YOUR BEST LIFE

The Term Living Your Best Life has been thrown around quite often, but how many of us know what it means? To some, it means having your dream home, dream car, dream vacation, etc. Notice that a dream always precedes what we want? And that is what it is: a dream. Surprisingly, we already have what we need. So, how do we start living this life and turn our dreams into reality? Some of you may have heard or even practiced some of what will be shared here, and for you, it serves as re-enforcement; for others, it will create awareness.

First, we need to find our purpose. We cannot proceed unless we know what that is. We thrive when we know what we are aspiring to. As a society, we have a problem with change or even starting over. Learn to embrace change because the more you resist, the more it persists. Understanding that, starting over, you are starting over with a great deal of experience and not from scratch, as we are programmed to believe. No one gets it right on the first try; life will always have difficulties, but we must be willing to take the good with the bad. We tend to be everything to everyone by taking on other people's stuff and losing ourselves in the process. Learn to say no and mean it—not maybe, or let me think about it— this is tough and takes practice. I am still working on myself.

"Ships don't sink because of the water around them; they sink because of the water that gets in them" (Anonymous). So, do not let what is happening around you get inside of you and weigh you down. We must find what matters to us—what is our priority—and stick with it. You may have heard the term, "We need to get uncomfortable to get comfortable." Step out of your comfort zone and take risks. Challenge yourself to be the best version of yourself you can be—emotionally, spiritually, and confidently. You will not know unless you try, and if you fail, it will be part of the learning process. Be like a river—keep moving. We are more capable than we let on, but we set up roadblocks through our thought processes. We need to get out of our way. There is always this fear that we will fail, but failure is part of the equation. No, it does not mean that it is over; it just means that this delay is propelling you towards greater things.

Our well-being is also optimal. 87% of our population is stressed, and this number will continue to rise. Understand that the things we fear the most will come upon us. Because everything we fear is a projection, and we are attracting it to ourselves. Every disappointment is an opening for a new appointment. Have you ever looked back and thought that something that you wanted so badly is of little significance now? The bottom line is that things are not happening to you; they are happening for you. This is a phrase that helped me handle conflicts, rejections, and resentments. It was evident when I applied for a job through an agency and was told I was not qualified, but when I saw the same job advertised, I applied and got it. Then, I was laid off, but I was placed in a new position before my actual termination date. And 24 years later, I am still with the company. In life, you will either be led to what is yours, or it will find you—it is that simple. Most of the time, the problem is not the problem; it is the way we think about it. Stop focusing on what you have no control over. We feel powerless when we are angry, become sick, struggle with our finances, or when others offend us. We have the power to steer our lives in the direction we want them to go. We are all gifted with internal powers that become unstoppable when we reclaim them.

No one else can give us joy, hope, money, the experience, or the existence we crave. Our first step is to be willing to make the change and stick with it.

We spend half our lives complaining—to ourselves and others about minute things and everything in between. The more you complain, the more things you will get to complain about. You must remain optimistic. Be in the here and now. Stop scattering your forces by talking about your affairs. Guard your mystic self. "Hold your personal stories close to your heart. Not everyone gets the privilege to know you." Debbie Lynn. Stop displaying your lives on social media. Work hard in silence, and let success make the noise. We are always one decision away from the next best thing—**BE PATIENT.** Patience is not only the ability to wait; it is how we conduct ourselves while waiting.

We all yearn for happiness and peace, but the mistake we make is to think that this is external. Happiness is our responsibility and no one else's. It will not come to you; it can only come from you—it cannot be outsourced. Reshape your thoughts to achieve happiness. Joy is external, but happiness is internal. Peace forces us to process life as it is and stop carving it out into what we want it to be.

Work on things no one can take from you-- your mindset, your character, your personality, and your entire being (Tiny Buddha).

Our mind is a powerful tool, and we must train it to be stronger than our emotions. We attract what we give a great deal of thought to. The first place we lose this battle is in our thinking. We are the masters of our minds; whatever we feed, it will cultivate. Do not hold thoughts of less than; instead, entertain thoughts that I deserve more. Stop being a victim of lack. We must raise our vibrations to attract what we want. The universe will only respond based on the frequency we are emitting. We will continue to recycle our experiences if we do not adjust our thought processes.

We all struggle, at some point, with **Self-Confidence**. We may be afraid to speak up for fear of repercussions, or we may be too meek to even try. I always tell my friends when we attend seminars or events that I am heading for a seat up front, and they would opt to sit in the back. My response is that if it does not have a reserved sign on those seats up front, then I am more than welcome to sit there. I also explained that choosing a seat in the back is a mindset they need to alter. Rosa Parks made it clear, at a time when it was forbidden, that she was not sitting in the back. Small steps such as this build your confidence. Who displays confidence, and dressing is a sure way of expressing that.

On the other side of the spectrum, another way to display self-confidence is to dress the way you want to be addressed. Have you noticed that a well-dressed person is more approachable? Why is that? We are always attracted to someone and believe that if they have self-esteem, they automatically have confidence. These are two extremely different social behaviors. An arrogant person will quickly claim that what they have is confidence----**Not!** We could also look at an introvert, whom you may think lacks confidence, but some introverts exert confidence when it is required. Even an extremely confident person at times exhibits doubt and withdrawal. This does not mean that they have lost it altogether; it just means that, as humans, we turn this on and off as we would a light switch, and this shows up in every aspect of our lives. There are folks who, no matter how hard they try, cannot embrace their self-confidence, and this is obvious when dealing with money.

Many of us feel that money is required to live a happy life. That is a myth. Money is a survival tool and nothing more. When we love money more than our integrity, then the lines get blurred. How many times do we see those who are wealthy lose all they have or are not happy? We give so much bravado to money that those who do not have enough are frowned upon. A poor man could be living a better life than a rich man, and you may question how that could be. Well, the poor man may be practicing and magnifying his core values and principles----Love, Acceptance, Compassion, and Forgiveness. Therefore, he attracts what he desires. Most use the money to gain and secure material wealth, and nothing is wrong with doing that. We are quick to judge a rich man, labeling him as greedy, but it is only true when he thinks he should have it all and no one else should. Consequently, if it is not shared with others or "given back," eventually the rich will be separated from their wealth, which solidifies the term "Want All, Lose All." Closed fists cannot receive the blessings or prosperity that are coming to them. From a biblical standpoint, we learn that the more we give, the more we receive. I cannot tell you how many times I share what I have, monetary and otherwise, and before the day is over, what is returned to me exceeds the amount I parted with. A co-worker of mine did not have enough on her MetroCard to get home. I gave her the last $10 I had that day. When I got home, there was a letter in my mailbox from my mortgage company. I was taken aback because I had made my monthly payment a few weeks prior. To my surprise, it was a refund totaling $500 for Escrow's coverage on my mortgage. It only took a few hours to realize my return. Be a pillar of support--be kind. Do not miss an opportunity to be of help to someone, nor should you turn down pleas for help if you are in the capacity to assist. Your return does not have to be monetary; it could be anything from getting a discount at your local store to finding the perfect parking space to getting a free upgrade to First Class. The more you give away, the more will be returned to you. You will look at someone and wonder why they are prospering and doing so well, and we tend to pass it off as luck, but luck has nothing to do with it. It is because they are practicing the Law of Compensation. You must do what is right to see things manifest in your favor.

Lots of error thoughts are attached to **money....**

> ➤ I do not deserve that much *money--stop denying* what is yours. What is due you will come to you.

- ➢ I will do better when I win the lottery—you are already a winner. Once you state that you do not have enough, you confirm a lack. This mindset is what lottery winners experience over and over as they watch their winnings dwindle into bankruptcy.
- ➢ Money is the root of all **evil—Money is an object—** *Lack* of money is the root of all evil. Therefore, the way we use money is where evil lies.
- ➢ Trying t**o Keep up with the Jones -** *I* am still curious as to who they are. Why compare yourself to a fictional character? Just do it, and everything will fall into place.
- ➢ Prosperity and Money are **synonymous -** *They are* not! Prosperity is not only about success and wealth. It is your birthright; therefore, it includes happiness and health as well. It is also apparent when you demonstrate a positive attitude.
- ➢ I will never have enough to pay my bills. When you start thinking of your bills as a service that provides comfort or the ability to purchase what you need instead of a burden, you will raise your vibration and thus manifest what you deserve.

We were not created to struggle or be unhappy. Learn to cultivate a prosperity consciousness. You must start thinking of yourself as a money magnet. These Affirmations will help attract the money you seek.

- ➢ Money flows to me effortlessly.
- ➢ The more I give away, the more it returns to me.
- ➢ I love money, and money loves me.
- ➢ I make money easily.

We need to stop talking negatively about ourselves. We tend to think and plan for the worst and do so with such determination, thus feeding our fears and anxieties. Turn this around and train your minds to focus on the best possible outcomes by allowing things to work out in time and restoring your peace. There is no doubt that "What you think you become, what you feel you attract, and what you imagine you create." (Buddha). If you think it is permanent, then it is; if you think you have reached your limit, then you have; if you think you will never get well, then you will not. You can see the correlation here. You must see everything as temporary. Never let the sadness of your past and the fear of your future ruin the happiness of your present. There is a reason why the rearview mirror of a car is smaller than the windshield. It is a reminder that what is going on behind you has little significance for what is ahead of you. Staying fixated on that rearview mirror, as we know it, leads to accidents. Focus on the windshield and embrace all that lies ahead. Do the things that make you feel good; invest in yourselves—so you can show up feeling good. Surround yourself with positive people and use positive words. See situations for how they are, not how you envision them in your mind.

> *Learn from it, but do not dwell on it.*
> *Energy flows where attention goes.*
> Practice forgiveness
> *Remain optimistic.*
> *Practice gratitude*

Success is always within our reach. At times, it does not happen as quickly as we would like. So, what do we do? We bloom where we are planted. Learn to work hard in silence and let success make the noise. You are right where you are meant to be. Stop forcing the process. When it is time for you to be elevated, it will happen so quickly that you will have no time to inject doubt into the process. In the meantime, make what you do interesting to others, and people will find you interesting. Know your worth. When you do, no one can make you feel worthless. We are always one decision away from our biggest breakthrough. On the other hand, do not stay where you are tolerated, strive to be somewhere you are appreciated. Also, do not resent others for their success; genuinely celebrate it and it will flow back to you. Instead of competition and comparison, practice gratitude and generosity.

You can rise from anything: -

> *Nothing is permanent.*
> *You have choices.*
> *You can train your mind to think new thoughts.*
> *You can create new habits.*
> *You can learn something new.*
> *You can completely recreate yourself.*
> *All that matters is that you decide and start the process.*

Learn to dream big! You are filled with greatness that has yet to evolve. Pursue your dream. Take a handle on life. Be exceptional, and dismiss the naysayers. Take risks. You are better and should do better. What you think is working against you is working for you. Failing is only in the mind. Take a confident approach to your life, then change your paradigm and reset your life. Once you raise your vibration, you will effortlessly attract the things you desire into your life. Permit yourself to shed who you used to be. This is your chance to PIVOT --- break free and bloom into your best self.

****

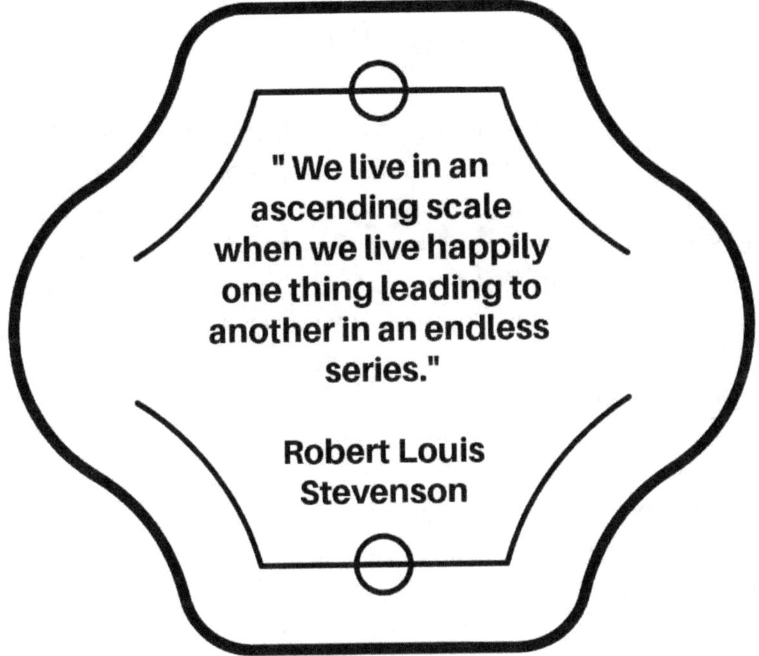
" We live in an
ascending scale
when we live happily
one thing leading to
another in an endless
series."

Robert Louis
Stevenson

Chapter 7
<u>ASCENDING</u>

The word Wellness popped up a lot during the pandemic, as we had no choice but to reflect on and incorporate it into our lives. I have even improved my game. To most of us, wellness means exercising and eating healthily, but there is something else we can add to the mix. It is what I call **M&Ms**. "No, not the ones that melt in your mouth, but not in your hands." I am referring to Meditation and Manifestation. I have realized that meditation consciously helps to become centered, minimize the chatter in our minds, and restore inner peace. Before practicing, I was all over the place---trying to be perfect, overthinking, a worry wart, and fearful of my shadow. I am sure most of you can relate to one or two of these traits. I was doing everything that was not keeping me centered. Meditation provides several benefits for our psychological well-being. It is not about morphing into a different person; it is about training your mind to put things into perspective. It is not a matter of switching off your thoughts or feelings but acknowledging them without judgment. The meditations I practice interchangeably are: -

Spiritual--This experience allows me to turn within and diminish all the judgments I have about myself until I am brought to a place of joy and peace.

Mindfulness—I focus on my breathing while inhaling and exhaling.

Focused -- Where I slow down my inner thoughts and become present in the moment. Practicing these will allow you to:

> Gain new perspectives on stressful situations.

> Develop skills to manage stress.

> Increase self-awareness.

> Be in the here and now, not hanging on to the past or yearning for the future.

> Reduce negative emotions.

> Increase your imagination and creativity.

> Increase your patience and tolerance.

I cherish meditation; it is a joy for me and such a wonderful space to be in.

Manifestation, on the other hand, will elevate you to a whole different level. I used to fear my thoughts because I had no control over them. Over time, I realized that manifestation helped to control these thoughts and that the Universe works in conjunction with them. For example, when I was planning to get a new car, like clockwork, I noticed the make and model cars I wanted kept showing up in ads and on the roadways. Or better yet, I thought of someone I had not heard from in a while, and unexpectedly, they were the person on the other end of my incoming call. Some of you may have experienced this or something similar, but it is not a coincidence or telepathy; it is the Universe responding to the energy and vibration that were emitted. Whatever you feed the universe, it will gladly return to you in the same form you project. Your thoughts become your reality, and, as Florence Scovel Shin states, "Your Word is your Wand." You must live with a mindset that you already have what you are seeking. A friend of mine was buying her first home, but her closing date kept changing. She became despondent and figured this was not meant to be. I directly told her to collect empty boxes and start packing. She was hesitant, but as soon as she started the process, she got the call with a new closing date. She has been living in her house now for 10+ years. When you focus on what you want, you will be drawn closer to it.

I keep a gratitude journal and find that the more I am grateful for, the more is given to me. Incorporating M&Ms, i.e., Meditation and Manifestation, into your daily routine will tremendously change your life. Looking back, I cannot fathom how destructive my thoughts were, and returning to that space no longer serves me. This auspicious turn of events has forced me to live in the moment and boldly face life as it is.

By focusing on what we want instead of things we do not want, the results are usually greater. We can be happy with little and miserable with much. Simplicity makes life more manageable, but we are creatures of habit who complicate things. Allowing others to focus on their own lives rids us of excessive burdens. Worrying, as we know it, causes us to repeat the same suffering. Learn to release what does not bring you peace. Practice forgiving yourself and others. Fear, worry, disappointment, and jealousy hold us back. They are also the culprits of many diseases. When we do not forgive, it is like taking poison and hoping the other person dies (Nelson Mandela). Releasing allows you to create space for the new to enter your life.

Once you get there, do not revert to being everything to everyone. How many of us are still stuck in this rut? You do not have to be super at anything. You just need someone to do things for you. It is not selfishness; it is self-care. Do the things that bring joy----travel, go to the gym, sleep late, go to the movies solo, go out to dinner solo—and look at these things as "Me Time." Celebrate yourself. Embrace your joy and protect your peace.

Change your environment and change your life. Learn to shift your perspective. Stop being ruled by emotions. Breathe, Mediate, and Pray. See things differently and revise as necessary.

- ➢ Cooperation instead of competition

- ➢ Unity instead of separation

- ➢ Harmony instead of Discord

- ➢ Inclusion instead of exclusion

Do not get triggered by someone's behavior, and do not let your ego get the best of you. If you are easily offended, then you can be easily manipulated. Everyone's journey is different. Accept and honor where you are on your journey.

Life is going to happen. Affirm your intent to release what no longer serves you. By doing so, you free up space for what will. Discard old patterns and beliefs. Be gentle and patient with yourself—be self-compassionate. You deserve harmony, balance, and peace. Boldly face your fears, and they will eventually fall by the wayside. Do not allow anyone to suck the winds out of your sails. You are on a mission, and the horizon awaits. Be brave, and be the light that attracts what you desire. Take responsibility---the outcome of your life is dependent on your thoughts and actions. Conscious efforts deliver what you seek. Develop a positive attitude. There is always something to be grateful for. Embrace change. Every change is an opportunity for growth. Dream big. Dreams do not have expiration dates; reinvent yourself at any age. Always be in the present---this is where your best self emerges.

When we profess love, we attract love. How often do we deny this one thing that is embedded in us? We chase love, shamelessly beg for love, become manipulative, hopelessly in love, and do things outside of our realm, all for the sake of love. These are all external actions. Turn it around by connecting to the love that is within us and watching miracles unfold. Learn to attract love--do not chase it!

Affirmations are not something that we wave a wand at, and it appears. It has great power and requires continuous practice. Be yourself and practice "I Am" affirmations:

> I am successful.

> I am worthy.

> I am healthy.

> I am confident.

> I am smart.

> I am kind.

We spend more than half our time caught up in external activities, thereby diminishing our thought process. Thoughts create an experience which determines the life we live. Watch your words---they are immensely powerful. Let go of the past. We seem to hang onto regrets and resentments like they are lifelines. Commit and make room for new things to come into your life. The universe has no bias; it does not recognize gender, race, religion, etc. It will respond exactly to what is presented to it. What you think about you bring about. If you wake up thinking you are going to have a bad day, you have already set the wheels in motion to deliver what you thought. Find a mantra that works for you. Mine is the song "Lovely Day" by Bill Withers. It always uplifts my spirit. Try it!

The only thing you have control over is your current thinking. Your thinking is where difficulties are born. Visualize down to the smallest details of what you seek. Function as if what you desire is already here—make preparations---welcome it—Live in the flow. The only way to reach your highest potential is to start believing that you have it. When you evolve, you give up what no longer serves you. You are the author of your life, and no one has power over you.

> ➢ Diminish negativity.

> ➢ Minimize complaining.

> ➢ Embrace positivity.

We do not praise ourselves enough. We find it easier to criticize ourselves and praise others. Speak loving words over your lives. Refrain from comparing yourself to others where you feel either superior or inferior. Love yourself unconditionally—you are enough. Approach everything and everyone with love. Be grateful for what you have, and do not yearn for what you do not have. Gratitude begets gratitude. Do not sit around and wait for something to happen; go out and make a change. Be excited about life—smile more, remove anything negative from your life, be excited about everything, and try new things. Take on that childlike demeanor. Notice that younger children are usually more happy than sad? We could do the same. Everything is temporary.

Life is an adventure that is filled with challenges. There are things that we can control, and there are others that are out of our control....

In Your Control:

> ➢ Your Thoughts

> ➢ Your Boundaries

> ➢ The goals you set.

> ➢ How you handle challenges

Out of Your Control:

> ➢ Others' opinions

> ➢ Your past and future

> ➢ The outcome of our efforts

> ➢ *What is occurring around you?*

We can determine a person's demeanor based on how they handle a crisis. Learn to switch your egos and wait a while before reacting. The benefits of doing so are great and will maintain your peace. Live in awe and wonder at what surrounds you. Notice how the moon glistens on the ocean, flowers bask in the sun, and birds entertain like a full orchestra. Make your lives just as magnificent as these acts. A child is always amazed at every discovery. Be as excited about life as they are in a candy store. We need to re-adopt these behaviors. When we do, our ego has no place to dwell.

Marvel at your life and celebrate how far you have come, mistakes and all. Each day, the sun stretches its arm across the globe. It does not seek permission to show up. Consequently, the Sun and Moon never compete as to who will shine brighter; they both shine when it is their turn. Learn from these acts of nature. Fall in love with yourself repeatedly. We all have a moral compass inside of us to make the right choice. We should take the time to listen. Know what to choose and what to give up. Nothing is in your way—we are the ones holding ourselves back. If you do not seize the opportunity now, would you prefer to live your life constantly yearning for what you need and eventually regretting that you should have struck while the iron was hot? The only way to reach your highest potential is to start believing that you have it. The world is your stage; let your performance leave a lasting impression on your audience. Go through life working on the LEGACY that you would like to be remembered for. A 747 aircraft cannot take off without moving. So, start your engines, engage

your throttle, and lift to the skies. When you evolve, you give up
what no longer serves you and **SOAR TO NEW HEIGHTS!**

The End

Final Words

Your takeaway from this book is to steer you toward becoming a better person whose life will transcend beyond your wildest imagination. You will radiate the love that is within you to all that you encounter. You will face life head-on and embrace all that is offered. It will allow you to throw caution to the wind--Be adventurous, be brave, and be that risk-taker. The more nervous you become about a situation or event, the more likely it is to transpire into something positive—be optimistic.

You are magnificent, powerful, deserving, and a force to be reckoned with. Time to Pivot---reclaim your power and let your light shine.

About the Author

Paulette Samuels lives in Queens, New York, and currently works in the Media industry. She is involved in Diversity, Equity, and Inclusion initiatives and received the Hearst INCLUDE Change Agent Certificate. She also worked in the financial sector and for a major airline. She has an MA in Media, Culture & Communication from New York University and a Persuasive Writing and Public Speaking Certificate from Harvard University. She is also a member of Toastmasters International. This is her first book, Titled "Time to Pivot and Do Something Different," ---a motivational compilation on how to navigate life. She is in tune with her subconscious self and practices gratitude by connecting with her spiritual being. When she is not giving Persuasive Speeches, and moderating Town Hall events, Paulette is a firm believer that "The World is her oyster, and her passport is her compass to finding her pearl."